Clark E. Moustakas is a faculty member of the Merrill-Palmer Institute in Detroit. He is also associated with other colleges and universities in workshops and seminars focusing on creativity and conformity, loneliness and individuality, child and family therapy, and human values and learning.

Dr. Moustakas is also the author of *Loneliness, Loneliness and Love, Creativity and Conformity, Psychotherapy with Children, The Authentic Teacher, Portraits of Loneliness and Love,* and is co-author with Cereta Perry of *Learning To Be Free.*

FINDING

YOURSELF

FINDING
OTHERS

clark e. moustakas

A SPECTRUM BOOK

RENTICE-HALL, INC., *Englewood Cliffs, New Jersey*

Library of Congress Cataloging in Publication Data

MOUSTAKAS, CLARK E
  Finding yourself, finding others.

  (A Spectrum Book)
  1. Identity (Psychology)   2. Self-actualization
(Psychology)   3. Interpersonal relations.   I. Title.
BF697.M673   158′.2   74-13128
ISBN 0-13-314708-8
ISBN 0-13-314674-X (pbk.)

FINDING YOURSELF, FINDING OTHERS
BY CLARK E. MOUSTAKAS

© 1974 BY PRENTICE-HALL, INC.
ENGLEWOOD CLIFFS, NEW JERSEY

A SPECTRUM BOOK

1 2 3 4 5 6 7 8 9 10

Printed in the United States of America

PRENTICE-HALL INTERNATIONAL, INC. (LONDON)
PRENTICE-HALL OF AUSTRALIA PTY., LTD. (SYDNEY)
PRENTICE-HALL OF CANADA, LTD. (TORONTO)
PRENTICE-HALL OF INDIA PRIVATE LIMITED (NEW DELHI)
PRENTICE-HALL OF JAPAN, INC. (TOKYO)

For Genevieve Driver

Quiet steady presence,
Vibrant light, joyous song.
Growing steadily,
with burst of energy and sparkling life.

Acknowledgments

I wish to thank Peg Hoddinott for all of her help, especially at urgent times when she responded enthusiastically and quickly; Mike Hunter, who assisted in selecting and placing illustrations and maintained a sense of humor in the midst of conflict and disagreement; and Mavis Wolfe for her skillful typing of the manuscript.

Special appreciation is also expressed to the following persons who shared with me their unpublished poems and their writings and gave me permission to include them in *Finding Yourself, Finding Others.*

"Can you sometimes," *by Miné Akanlar Boyd*
"To communicate is the beginning," *by Nancy Ceranowicz*
letter, *by Vian Catrell*
unpublished paper, *by James A. Gold*
"Look at me. Please see me." and "Surrounded by glass," *by Peg Hoddinott*
letter, *by Paul Jensen*
"Strict vine tied me up," *by Kazuko Yoshinaga Ibachi*
excerpt from "Autonomous Motivation," *by Dorothy Lee*
"Upregard," *by Julie Mills*
excerpts from "By way of tragedy," *by Ross Mooney*

Acknowledgment is accorded the following authors and sources of publications with reference to poems and excerpts included in the book:

Reprinted from *A Death in the Family* by James Agee. Copyright © 1957 by James Agee Trust. Reprinted by permission of the publisher, Grosset & Dunlap, Inc.

"A Theoretical Model for Personality Studies" by Andras Angyal. *Journal of Personality,* September 1951, Copyright 1951 by Duke University Press.

Cibecue Apache by Keith Basso. Published by Holt, Rinehart, Inc., 1970.

The Sound of Silence by Raymond John Baughan. Copyright © 1965 by Raymond John Baughan. Reprinted by permission of Beacon Press.

The Disowned Self by Nathaniel Branden. Nash Publishers, Los Angeles, California, 1971.

Between Man and Man by Martin Buber. London: Routledge & Kegan Paul Ltd., 1947.

From *Soul On Ice* by Eldridge Cleaver. Copyright © 1968 by Eldridge Cleaver. Used with permission of McGraw-Hill Book Company.

I: 6 Non-Lectures by E. E. Cummings. Copyright 1962. Reprinted by permission of publishers, Harvard University Press.

"somewhere i have never travelled" by E. E. Cummings. Copyright 1931, 1959, by E. E. Cummings. Reprinted from his volume, *Complete Poems 1913–1962,* by permission of Harcourt Brace Jovanovich, Inc.

The Mind as Nature by Loren Eiseley. Published by Harper & Row, 1962.

"Dynamics, Existence and Values" by Victor Frankl. *Journal of Existential Psychiatry* Vol. 2, #5, 1961.

"Therapeutic Procedures with Schizophrenic Patients" by Eugene Gendlin. From *Theory and Practice of Psychotherapy with Specific Disorders* edited by Max Hammer. Charles C. Thomas, publisher, 1972.

Sand and Foam by Kahlil Gibran. Published by Alfred A. Knopf, Inc., 1962.

Excerpts from "Goody-by, Little Boy!" by H. Gordon Green, *The Reader's Digest,* September, 1963. Copyright 1963 by the Reader's Digest Assn., Inc.

"Individual In Management" by Robert S. Hartman. The Nationwide Management Center.

"Attitude Organization in Elementary School Classrooms" by Jules Henry. *American Journal of Orthopsychology.* XXVII, #1, January, 1957.

Demian by Herman Hesse. Copyright 1925 by S. Fischer Verlag. Copyright © 1965 by Harper & Row, Publishers, Inc. Reprinted by permission of publisher.

"The Search of Glory" by Karen Horney. From *The Self* edited by Clark Moustakas. Published by Harper & Row, Inc. 1956.

"Finding the Real Self," a letter with a foreword by Karen Horney. *The American Journal of Psychoanalysis* 1949, Volume IX.

(continued on page 119)

1

REMAINING ALIVE AS A PERSON

When words come of themselves, they are alive, they flow easily. When they are forced or questioned, they cease to be spontaneous, real expressions. Words that stem from inner life flow like the rhythms and seasons, like the river, like the song of the Eskimo in the deep breath he takes:

The great sea
Has set me adrift
It moves me
As the weed in a great river.
Earth and the great weather
Move me
Have carried me away
And move my inward parts with joy.

I do not know whether you can stay with me in the way in which I have decided to share my life with others but if you can I offer something of myself that may create currents in your own awareness and being.

C. M.

My message is not simply in words and pictures but in the pauses between, in the sweep of feeling and melody, in the mystery through which life is created. If I were interested merely in providing you with knowledge about something, I would summarize in brief terms. But there is a crucial difference between a living expression and knowledge that is abstracted from life.

Perhaps there is no tangible or concrete way to create the essence of what it means to be your own self and to connect fundamentally with other human beings. Sometimes in a spontaneous, exuberant rush of feelings, the words form, and the body comes alive. But in that instant I catch a glimpse of others and stop—it is a moment frozen by the presence of neutral and lifeless people. Whatever comes then has lost its power of movement and impact. Right in the middle of a flowing breath—the question, the frown, the disapproving glance; or just the indifferent or neutral face. I know then that I am not meeting the preconceptions of others. I am not following the path of expectations. But I stand on my own ground and, however difficult, I listen to the sounds within to discover what it means to stay alive as an individual.

Feelings are naturally connected to body behavior, but under a system of restriction and repression the body gradually freezes and the individual becomes molded and stereotyped. Unique dialect, intonation, and natural body rhythms are destroyed. In a system that defines and rewards the appropriate, the individual becomes robotlike, muscles become tense, holding back the rage, the crying out against the poisons, both visible and invisible, that surround the person. In contrast, the individual who is growing with the freedom and dignity of unique selfhood experiences a range of feelings that are clearly marked by body expressions, as in the Eskimo song: Fear is the tightening of the sinews; anger, the loosening of the bowels; and joy, floating viscera.

C. M.

4

The serious thing for each person to recognize vividly and poignantly, each for himself, is that every falling away from species-virtue, every crime against one's own nature, every evil act, *every one without exception records itself* in our unconscious and makes us despise ourselves. Karen Horney had a good word to describe this unconscious perceiving and remembering; she said it "registers." And it registers *in our books!* If we do something we are ashamed of it registers to our discredit, and if we do something honest or fine or good it registers to our credit. The net results ultimately are either one or the other—either we respect and accept ourselves or we despise ourselves and feel contemptible, worthless, and unlovable. Theologians used to use the word *accidie* to describe the sin of failing to do with one's life all that one knows one can do.

A. H. MASLOW

5

Look at me. Please, see me
Not my clothes or stubby nails
Or homely face.
Open your heart, so you can see mine.
I do not ask you to agree with
Or understand all you see
For I don't even do that.
Just look at what is really there
And allow it to be.

PEG HODDINOTT

Individuality and identity emerge from the deep levels of the self, from the resources and talents that exist in each of us to be formed and shaped into a particular being in the world. It is these values which society should recognize, encourage, and affirm. The self cannot develop unless there is freedom, choice, and responsibility, unless each person experiences his own senses and becomes an active force in life, free to choose and select, free to feel and express openly and honestly the nature of these feelings, free to identify with alive persons who encourage growth in individual identity, who value being for itself, and who can enable the person to engage himself and be committed to meaningful activity.

C. M.

. . . If I were to list the most important learning experiences in my life, there come to mind getting married, discovering my life work, having children, getting psychoanalyzed, the death of my best friend, confronting death myself, and the like. I think I would say that these were more important learning experiences for me than my Ph.D. or any 15 or 150 credits of any courses that I've ever had. I certainly learned more about *myself* from such experiences. I learned, if I may put it so, to throw aside many of my "learnings," that is, to push aside the habits and traditions and reinforced associations which had been imposed upon me. Sometimes this was at a very trivial, and yet meaningful, level. I particularly remember when I learned that I really hated lettuce. My father was a "nature boy," and I had lettuce two meals a day for the whole of my early life. But one day in analysis after I had learned that I carried my father inside me, it dawned on me that it was my father, through *my* larynx, who was ordering salad with every meal. I can remember sitting there, realizing that *I* hated lettuce and then saying, "My God, take the damn stuff away!" I was emancipated, becoming in this small way me rather than my father.

A. H. MASLOW

Mother To Son

Well, Son, I'll tell you
Life for me ain't been no crystal stair.
It's had tacks in it,
And splinters,
And boards torn up,
And places with no carpets on the floor.

Bare.
But all the time
I'se been climbin' on
And reachin' landin's
And turning corners
And sometimes goin' on in the dark
Where there ain't been no light.
So, Boy, don't you turn back.
Don't you set down on the steps
'Cause you find it's kinder hard.
Don't you fall now—
For I'se still goin', Honey,
I'se still climbin'
And life for me ain't been
      no crystal stair.

    LANGSTON HUGHES

My pilgrimage of repeated return to the sea will not end so long as I live. And now I know that I *shall* live, for as long as is given to me. And should my body be battered even more, then I will live as I can, enjoying what I might, having what joy is available to me, and being what I may to the people whom I love. I must continue my pilgrimage, for it is my only way of remaining open to this vision. It is to this end that I must struggle for the remainder of that pilgrimage that is my life.

Along the way, like everyone else, I must bear my burdens. But I do *not* intend to bear them graciously, nor in silence. I will take my sadness and as I can I will make it sing. In this way when others hear my song, they may resonate and respond out of the depths of their own feelings.

We will call out to each other in the darkness of the Great Forest, so that we may not be lost to one another. Then, like the innocent Forest People, for a moment we will live in a world created by a God so benevolent that, when there is trouble, we will know that He must be asleep. And, like the Hasidim, just when life is heaviest with pain and anguish, that is the time when we will dance and sing together to waken the sleeping God of our own lost hope.

SHELDON KOPP

2

ORIGINS OF SELFHOOD

Whatever the conditions under which a child grows up he will, if not mentally defective, learn to cope with others in one way or another and he will probably acquire some skills. But there are also forces in him which he cannot acquire or even develop by learning. You need not, and in fact cannot, teach an acorn to grow into an oak tree, but when given a chance, its intrinsic potentialities will develop. Similarly the human individual, given a chance, tends to develop his particular human potentialities. He will develop then the unique alive forces of his real self; the clarity and depth of his own feelings, thoughts, wishes, interests; the ability to tap his own resources, the strength of his will power; the special capacities or gifts he may have; the faculty to express himself and to relate himself to others with his spontaneous feelings. All this will in time enable him to find his set of values and his aims in life. In short, he will grow, substantially undiverted, toward self-realization. And that is why I speak now of the real self as that central inner force, common to all human beings and yet unique in each, which is the deep source of growth.

KAREN HORNEY

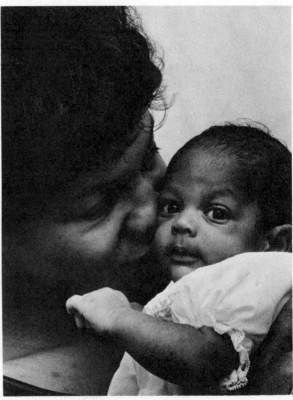

Every individual, from the moment of birth, is unique, un-like any other being who has ever existed. From the environment, nourishment and care are required to satisfy biological needs and to maintain life, but no one is rooted solely in physical re-quirements, waiting passively to be aroused to states of tension, and then actively seeking to reduce these tensions in order to achieve a state of rest. From the beginning, the infant reaches out into the world, alert, active, directed, expressive. Congenital activity and other signs of preference and selectivity are early forms of self-expression and identity.

C. M.

Let me first speak about the infant. . . . Unlike many of us, he *knows* what he likes and dislikes, and the origin of these value choices lies strictly within himself. He is the center of the valuing process, the evidence for his choices being supplied by his own senses. He is not at this point influenced by what his parents think he should prefer, or by what the church says, or by the opinion of the latest "expert" in the field, or by the persuasive talents of an advertising firm. It is from within his own experiencing that his organism is saying in non-verbal terms—"This is good for me." "That is bad for me." "I like this." "I strongly dislike that." He would laugh at our concern over values, if he could understand it. How could anyone fail to know what he liked and disliked, what was good for him and what was not?

CARL R. ROGERS

Gardner Murphy has described the child's world as a process of reaching out, relating and discovering:

They will immerse themselves in the world; they soak themselves in its rich qualities. Its endless problems and challenges are intrinsically appealing. Now and then it hurts them, and they learn how to avoid the recurrence of such hurts; but in general it is a rich and commanding world which they must understand and with which they must come to terms. Often the child has to be dragged from his sensory and motor satisfactions to swallow the food which adults think necessary to meet his "primary needs," or dragged to bed against the competition of excitations which stimulate his sense organs and later his imagination. Human nature, as directly observed, is no matter of viscera alone. It is a matter of exploring the possibility of surfaces, lines, colors, and tones and, later on, the symphonies, mountains and stars.

GARDNER MURPHY

The young child trusts his own senses to confirm or deny, to lead to harmony and fit; he cries out in protest against the thwarting, alienating, unfitting dimensions of the environment. By perceptual and sensual contacts and freedom of movement, the young child participates in life, choosing the fitting and rejecting that which is not in harmony, that which does not create a sense of well-being, continuity, and fulfillment. From the beginning, there is "Yes" and "No" in the individual's response to life.

C. M.

The real self—that central inner core within each person—is the most stable and consistent value in life. To live in terms of the person we are is the only way to healthy self-fulfillment. Being authentic permits us to establish a personal identity, and fosters genuine human relations.

C. M.

3

BEING AN INDIVIDUAL

The life of any person or thing is the person's own. Others can and do affect the environment in which potentialities can be fulfilled, but in real growth the individual alone determines the direction and what is true in his world. Tenderness, caring, affirmation, all affect the person in the development of uniqueness and in the enhancement of the self, but ultimately the person alone is responsible for who he chooses to be and how he actualizes potentialities.

C. M.

The presence of the person ensures an awakening, a personal process that involves an answering engagement with life. We must learn to talk to the powers of the self as the Apache do.

Our songs come from those inner powers. We keep them alive when we sing to them. *That* way a power knows you are trying to tell it something. It knows when it hears your songs. And when a power hears your songs it wants to listen. If you don't sing your songs, but somebody else's, then a power won't know where to find you; it won't know how to work for you.

C. M.

Every individual embodies and contains a uniqueness, a reality, that makes him unlike any other person or thing. To maintain this uniqueness in the face of threats and pressures, in times of shifting patterns and moods, is the ultimate challenge and responsibility of every man. In creative experience, perception is unique; there is a sense of wholeness, unity, and centeredness. In such moments, man is immersed in the world, exploring, spontaneously expressing himself, and finding satisfaction in being rooted in life as a whole person. When man is intimately related to life, he neither ties himself to restricted goals that he must pursue; nor is he confined by directions and instructions and rules, or restrained by conditioned responses and techniques. He is free; he is open; he is direct; he encounters life with all of his resources; and he lives in accordance with the unique requirements of each situation as it unfolds before him. Neither bounded by the past, nor fixed to the present, the creative person transcends the limits of history and time by realizing new facets of himself and by relating to the demands of existence in new ways.

C. M.

Spontaneity is another component of individuality. It involves a certain quality of imagination, daring, and risk, a forward-moving quality of the self, in which an individual plunges into new areas, tries out new experiences, and ventures into the unknown. In spontaneous moments the individual simply lets go, freely, with his whole self, as an artist throws himself into a painting or a jazz musician creates his theme, as an infant immerses himself in the world of shape and color and movement.

C. M.

Spontaneity means losing one's self as a separate other yet remaining absolutely related to the moment, whether in poetry or dance or music or an idea, or even in meditation and silence. One lets go of external structure, of extraneous rules, of the system, and in doing so, while the controlling, conscious side is lost, the uniqueness of the individual, the most distinctive characteristics of the self, shine forth. Then the reality being experienced is a personal reality based on one's own senses, like seeing for the first time; then the individual is not determined by others but only by his own experience.

C. M.

But if poetry is your goal, you've got to forget all about punishments and all about rewards and all about self-styled obligations and duties and responsibilities etcetera ad infinitum and remember one thing: that it's you—nobody else—who determine your destiny and decide your fate. Nobody else can be alive for you; nor can you be alive for anybody else.

E. E. CUMMINGS

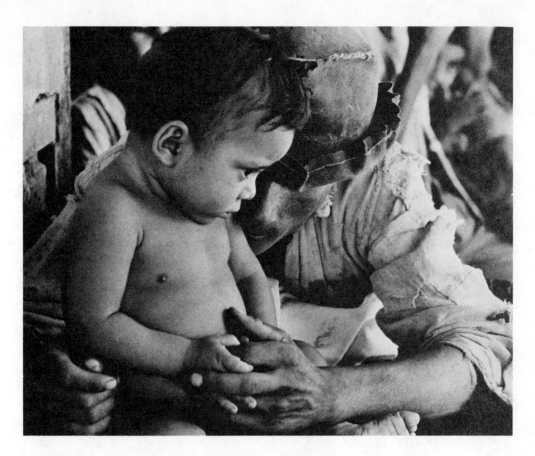

What a real living human being is made of seems to be less understood today than at any time before, and men—each one of whom represents a unique and valuable experiment on the part of nature—are therefore shot wholesale nowadays. If we were not something more than unique human beings, if each one of us could really be done away with once and for all by a single bullet, storytelling would lose all purpose. But every man is more than just himself; he also represents the unique, the very special and always significant and remarkable point at which the world's phenomena intersect, only once in this way and never again. That is why every man's story is important, eternal, sacred; that is why every man, as long as he lives and fulfills the will of nature, is wondrous, and worthy of every consideration. In each individual the spirit has become flesh, in each man the creation suffers, within each one a redeemer is nailed to the cross.

HERMANN HESSE

25

Every human being has the chance of changing at any instant. There is the freedom to change, in principle, and no one should be denied the right to make use of it. Therefore, we never can predict a human being's future except within the large frame of a statistical survey referring to a whole group. On the contrary, an individual personality is essentially unpredictable. The basis for any predictions would be represented by biological, psychological or sociological influences. However, one of the main features of human existence is the capacity to emerge from and rise above all such conditions—to transcend them. By the same token, man is ultimately transcending himself. The human person then transcends himself insofar as he reshapes his own character.

VIKTOR E. FRANKL

To communicate is the beginning
of understanding. To feel is the
beginning of self-growth. To
touch is the beginning of involvement. To love, the beginning of
all that will ever be.
 I breathe and I grow. A
flickering candle flame can be
my world. My candle light touches
softly and gently from a distance
till it draws you, and your face
is glowing in the light.
 My candle dances, and I will
        always

NANCY CERANOWICZ

Many times in my life I have been faced with a dilemma that, after much internal struggle and deliberation, turned out to be illusory. I continually discovered that only one pathway was open, that there was only one way to go—a way that grew out of my own self. The problem turned out to be not one of resolving a situation that called for choosing among alternatives, but rather a question of bring into being what already existed as self-potential, that is, it required bringing into being my own identity as it related to the challenge of a crucial situation. It is this experience of expressing and actualizing one's individual identity in communion with one's self, with nature, and with other persons that I call creative. Growth of individual identity in open relatedness; creation of being in vital experiences with other beings; ingestion of meaning, feeling, belief, value, within a unique self—this is the essential creativity of human life.

C. M.

We must not accept as intrinsic the antagonism between individual interests and social interests. A. H. Maslow has strongly emphasized that this kind of antagonism exists only in a sick society. Individual and social interests are synergetic, not antagonistic; thus, creative individual expression results in social creativity and growth—which in turn encourages and frees the individual to further self-expression and discovery. Individuality must be encouraged, not stifled. What is true and of value to society can emerge only from genuine self-interest.

C. M.

4

THE PATH
OF
ALIENATION

From the moment of birth, when the stone-age baby first confronts its twentieth-century mother, the baby is subjected to forces of outrageous violence, called love, as its mother and father have been, and their parents and their parents before them. These forces are mainly concerned with destroying most of the baby's potentialities. This enterprise is on the whole successful. By the time the new human being is fifteen or so, we are left with a being like ourselves, a half-crazed creature, more or less adjusted to a mad world. This is normality in our present age.

R. D. LAING

The origins of alienation are a lack of recognition and love in childhood; obedience to external "shoulds" rather than to the preferences of the inner self; the absence of a growing identity that comes from self-choices; and judgment of oneself on the basis of the evaluations of others. Alienation is a retreat away from self-awareness and toward self-anesthesia where one's own senses are denied as valid and feelings are no longer felt and owned.

C. M.

Alienation, that is, the developing of a life outlined and determined by others, rather than a life based on one's own inner experience, soon leads to desensitization. The individual stops trusting his own feelings and, since he cannot actually make another's feeling his own, he learns mechanically or automatically to make the proper gestures or facial expressions to denote the appropriate feelings: a smile is not a smile, joy is not joy, and sadness is not sadness; the movements of the face and body are properly placed to take on the appearance of the appropriate emotions. The alienated person is anesthetized; he is embedded in a world without color, without excitement, without risk and danger, without mystery—without meaning. It is only one step from here to self-abnegation, when the person, without awareness, renounces himself and becomes the conformist the outside world expects him to be.

C. M.

In the idiom of games theory, people have a repertoire of games based on particular sets of learned interactions. Others may play games that mesh sufficiently to allow a variety of more or less stereotyped dramas to be enacted. The games have rules, some public, some secret. Some people play games that break the rules of games that others play. Some play undeclared games, so rendering their moves ambiguous or downright unintelligible, except to the expert in such secret and unusual games. Such people, prospective neurotics or psychotics, may have to undergo the ceremonial of a psychiatric consultation, leading to diagnosis, prognosis, prescription. Treatment would consist in pointing out to them the unsatisfactory nature of the games they play and perhaps teaching new games. A person reacts by despair more to loss of the *game* than to sheer "object loss," that is, to the loss of his partner or partners as real persons. The maintenance of the game rather than the identity of players is all important.

R. D. LAING

When next I feel those steel fingers close around my heart I must seek a division of self, must find a way of turning around inside, as it were, to discover those pale blue eyes still fixed upon me, and to reject at last the ancient accusation, must face my father who now is the condemning part of self, and say, "It is *you* who is the enemy, not those out there. It is *you* who would destroy me!"

In danger I will feel either fear or anger, and either may be self-preserving. If I am to avoid danger by running, fear will help me run faster; if I am to stand my ground, anger will help me stand it more firmly. In this neurotic danger, since I intend not to run, fear is useless, worse than useless, is itself the greatest hazard. Anger is what I need. To cringe before that inner denunciation is to perpetuate the past, to reaffirm my father's authority to determine how I regard myself. All these years his judgment has held sway; now I must find a way, without tearing the whole house down, to rise up against him, to seek him out who now is part of me, who still wordlessly condemns me as unworthy. If I have something to say and mean it I must stand behind it, must mobilize a dark and deep-running anger to protect it.

ALAN WHEELIS

Self-betrayal means that the person does not use his own faculties in determining which experiences contribute to self-realization and which are irrelevant or impeding; the person no longer uses his own powers and organs to create reality and venture into new life. He forces himself to fit into another person's plans and to do work that has no meaning or value. Thus he does not trust his own immediate experience and he is neither open to himself nor to the world. Betrayal of self-values occurs initially through rejection; the rejection may be direct and hostile or it may be devious and duplicitous. The rejection of the individual often begins when ambitious parents (and later teachers) set up goals and communicate expectations, either directly or deceptively, so that what they really want and expect from the child registers at subliminal levels regardless of what they say. Sometimes adults program the child's life with incentives and rewards so that he progresses step by step toward their definitions, toward their goals, toward their expected achievements. In the process the unique child as a growing person is canceled out and what remains is a definition, a role, a mechanical man, that takes its direction from external judgments and cues. In other words, the self of the child is eliminated from daily existence. A young woman in a letter to Karen Horney describes the process:

How is it possible to lose a self? The treachery, unknown and unthinkable, begins with our secret psychic death in childhood— if and when we are not loved and are cut off from our spontaneous wishes. (Think: What is left?) But wait—it is not just this simple murder of a psyche. That might be written off, the tiny victim might even "outgrow" it—but it is a perfect double crime in which he himself also gradually and unwittingly takes part. He has not been accepted for himself, as he is.

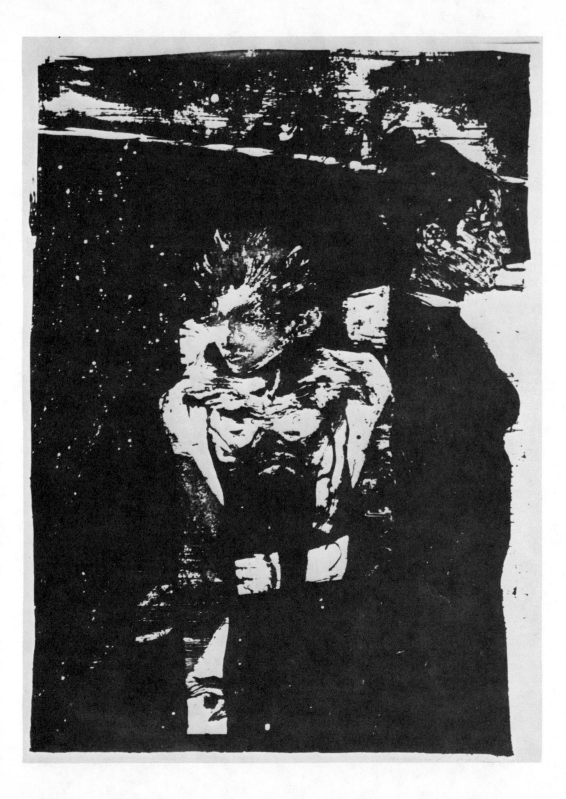

Or, they "love" him, but they want him or force him or expect him to be different! Therefore he must be unacceptable. He himself learns to believe it and at last even takes it for granted. He has truly given himself up. No matter now whether he obeys them, whether he clings, rebels or withdraws—his behavior, his performance is all that matters. His center of gravity is in "them," not in himself—yet if he so much as noticed it he'd think it natural enough. And the whole thing is entirely plausible; all invisible, automatic, and anonymous!

C. M.

. . . I once knew a brilliant and discerning philosopher who spent many hours each week alone in movie houses watching indifferently pictures of a quality far below his actual intellectual tastes. I knew him as an able, friendly, and normal person. Somewhere behind his sunny mask, however, he was in flight, from what, I never knew. Was it job, home, family—or was it rather something lost that he was seeking? Whatever it was, the pictures that passed before his eyes, the sounds, only half-heard, could have meant little except for an occasional face, a voice, a fading bar of music. No, it was the darkness and the isolation he wanted, something in the deep night of himself that called him home.

LOREN EISLEY

When betrayal of the self occurs through duplicity, the individual is caught up in a double-bind. The message communicated by parents and teachers is twofold and contradictory. Outwardly these adults are saying that they respect the child's own perceptions, interests, and preferences, but at the same time another message is being conveyed: namely, that they prefer and expect the child to conform to their own wishes and standards. Outwardly the words sound affirmative and accepting, but inwardly there is a range of bodily tensions and meanings which are also communicated. Duplicity enters the situation and is a form of betrayal when parents and teachers do not say what they mean—that is, when they say one thing but mean another—or when words and feelings are in opposition in the same person, or when any contradictory series of messages is being communicated from adult to child.

C. M.

The ultimate consequence of betrayal of the self is alienation and inauthenticity. The young person searching for identity and self-affirmation, lacking recognition, and threatened by the withdrawal of love, launches into an alien life. The spontaneous, genuine self is replaced by a controlled, calculating self-system dominated by the rules and "shoulds" of the adult world. The original self-awareness becomes self-deception and the individual no longer realizes that the real self has been abnegated in favor of a substitute. Alienated individuals wear masks that bear no resemblance to the real face underneath, carry out functions and roles that have no personal significance or meaning, and, in general, engage in daily pretenses that are far removed from authentic life.

C. M.

One important way in which the self-determination of a person may be impaired is by trading the birthright of mastery over his own destiny for the mess of pottage of protection—and dependency. In addition to the assumption of his weakness, an over-evaluation of the power of his parents and of the protection which they can give induces the child to make this fatal bargain. The terms of the bargain are set, at least by implication: "You are weak and helpless against the world which is full of dangers; if you are good, if you do what we want you to do, and don't follow your impulses, we will take care of you and protect you."

ANDRAS ANGYAL

One of the most striking characteristics of American culture has been the phenomenon of intragroup aggression, which finds its pathological purity of expression in witch hunts. It comes as a frightening surprise to democratic people to find themselves suddenly in terror of their neighbors; to discover that they are surrounded by persons who carry tales about others while confessing evil of themselves; to perceive a sheeplike docility settling over those whom they considered strong and autonomous. In this witch's brew destructive criticism of others is the toad's horns; docility the body of the worm; feelings of vulnerability the chicken heart; fear of internal (intragroup) hostility the snake's fang; confession of evil deeds the locust's leg; and boredom and emptiness the dead man's eye. The witch-hunt syndrome is thus stated to be a dynamically interrelated system of feelings and actions made up of destructive criticism of others, docility, feelings of vulnerability, fear of internal aggression, confession of evil deeds, and boredom.

JULES HENRY

Surrounded by glass,
I search for my place
In a world of laughter
And tears.

Longing to join them
Isn't enough
I can not break the glass
When you finally open the door
Will it be too late?

PEG HODDINOTT

40

The labels we attach to people, the names and all the other things that identify the individual by distinguishing him from the masses, are just what prevent genuine knowing. For labels and classifications make it appear that we know the other, when actually we have caught the outline and not the substance. Since we are convinced we know ourselves and others, since we take this knowledge for granted, we fail to recognize that our perceptions are often only habits growing out of routines and familiar forms of expression. We no longer actually see what is happening before us and in us, and, not knowing that we do not know, we make no effort to be in contact with the real. We continue to use labels to stereotype ourselves and others, and these labels have replaced human meanings, unique feelings, and growing life within and between persons.

C. M.

The conforming person is often the "good" person whose primary mode of existence is rooted in others; the "other" becomes the center of the world. It requires intelligence to know what another expects of you, to be aware of the other's values and preferences; it requires intelligence to develop reactive abilities, to know what other people want and believe and care about. And the most intelligent persons are apt to be the most successful in tuning in on others' requirements and expectations and in achieving the approved goals.

Submission and telling people what they want to hear are rewarded with attention, recognition, approval, privilege, and status, but there is a price to pay in loss of self-esteem, personal integrity, and meaning in living. As long as the right signs are given from the outside, as long as someone is conditioning the person for what is expected and rewarding him for doing the right things, he appears to be comfortable, secure, and content. But as soon as there is no external stimulation and direction, as soon as external rewards cease to have meaning, the person becomes confused, for, having given up his own individuality, his own response to life, he experiences little knowledge of who he is, what he wants, and what his real feelings are. Such a person has lost touch with the actual both in himself and in others; he is unable to distinguish between the genuine and the counterfeit.

C. M.

Many factors enter into the absence of meaning and genuine warmth in communication. These include a social and institutional climate that encourages and supports anonymity, intellectualization, and role playing. Fear often prevents the person from overcoming and transcending the consequences of conditioning. Of all the forms of fear—fear of being misunderstood, of being diminished, of becoming vulnerable—none is more thwarting than the fear of rejection. For most people partial communication and relationship are preferred to the risks of honesty and openness of self-expression and self-disclosure.

C. M.

Unfortunately, there is much in life to interfere with authentic development of the self—the humdrum of everday living, drifting with convention, being stuck in rules and regulations instead of openly meeting life, yielding to pressures, compromising, doing the expected, and everything that passes for morality, particularly the superficial cliches and rules of convention and propriety. Other forces that hinder the development of the self include playing a role, doing one's duty, and the interpretation and analysis of people and events. In general, all efforts and actions directed toward looking behind reality, explaining, and justifying its existence, interfere with direct, primary, authentic experience. The authentic person, rooted in himself and not imprisoned in a system of fixed procedures, policies, and regulations, does not analyze and explain reality; he engages in it freely, openly, immediately, spontaneously. In this way, he achieves new integrations, new meanings, and growing actualizations of his own identity.

C. M.

Intellectuality today is overstressed and overused and, in exaggerated forms, stifles creativity and spontaneity. When intelligence is used to establish rigid systems and hierarchies, when it becomes a substitute for human concern and human involvement, when intellectual values are more important than self-values, they then become destructive, violating individual integrity and human decency. The system—any system which chooses intelligence over morality—is rooted in mechanics and laws which, basically, are no more than the values of authoritarian individuals who prefer death to life, submission to courage, routines and habits to inventiveness and ingenuity, and, on the whole, anything that passes for order, efficiency, and organization.

C. M.

The alienated individual experiences a constant vague sense of anxiety. Life is brief, time passes, and the authentic sources of being are drying up. More and more the limit of time becomes a threatening realization, and a sense of incompleteness and despair often overwhelms the person. This is the despair of self-abrogation and self-denial. Kierkegaard in a terse, moving passage, describes the despair of self-denial in his book, *The Sickness Unto Death:*

A despairing man is in despair over something. So it seems for an instant, but only for an instant, that same instant the true despair manifests itself, or despair manifests itself in its true character. For in the fact that he despaired of something, he really despaired of himself, and now would be rid of himself. Thus when the ambitious man whose watchword was "Either Caesar or nothing" does not become Caesar, he is in despair thereat. But this signifies something else, namely, that precisely because he did not become Caesar he now cannot endure to be himself . . . In a profounder sense it is not the fact that he did not become Caesar which is intolerable but the self which did not become Caesar is the thing that is intolerable; or, more correctly, what is intolerable to him is that he cannot get rid of himself. . . .

C. M.

In conformity, life has no meaning for there is no true basis for existence. Cut off from his own real wishes and capacities, the individual experiences no fulfillment and no sense of authentic relatedness. He strives to achieve safety and status. He strives to overcome his natural desires and to gain a victory over his natural surroundings. His goals are acquisition and control. Separated from nature and others yet appearing to be in harmony with them, he takes his cues from the designated authority figures. A young woman in psychotherapy has recognized this pattern:

So you have to put everything out . . . as a question, you know. Because he's the one who knows and we're the ones who don't know. You can't—you're sort of stepping onto his territory if you start giving out with pronouncements of facts. You see, what you're doing is you're competing, you're being disrespectful. You're moving into his position which—you just don't *do that. . . . And I know that very well, but how I know it or why I know it— you see, I don't know it as intellectual concept—I just* know *it. My father didn't allow anybody but himself to be the law-giver and statement maker. . . . And a lot of those things I know, I don't know in words, I just know.*

C. M.

When we are not honest, we are not all there. That part of us which if expressed would make us whole is buried, and a false, distorted image replaces the real self. At first the individual is aware of the distortions between the real self and his stated thoughts and feelings, but, with repeated experience, self-awareness slips into self-deception and the individual no longer knows what is fantasy and what is reality. There is an additional tragedy: others are taken in by the lie and the dishonesty spreads and leads to profound and inevitable anguish and destruction.

C. M.

5

IN SEARCH
OF
SELF

Through some sudden event, some crisis, some abrupt change, what a person has known and counted on ceases to be. A pattern of life is broken. Alienation results, not only because the individual is cut off from what he knows, but also because he questions the reality of his past experience, the reality of what he has perceived and valued and loved. He discovers that a relationship is not as he saw it, that what he regarded as real did not exist. And this shattering insight calls into doubt the reality of his entire life. From such a realization comes despair and disillusion. A search begins, a search for order and harmony in a universe that now appears to be flighty, unstable, and capricious.

C. M.

51

The moment for initiating an authentic life and departing from betrayal and alienation is always present. No matter how entrenched a person is in the world of the other, in rationalizing, in analyzing, in intellectualizing, no matter how immersed in standards and values and goals of the system, he still can, in the next moment, decide to alter the course of his life. He still can become the one he really is, creating meanings and values and actualizing potentialities that are consistent with his real self. No one can take this away. And for any particular person, no one can predict what the individual will do. Regardless of his past, in any situation the person can choose to activate real directions of the self. It is true for every individual that at any moment he can choose to become himself, which is the only way to authentic existence.

C. M.

When the persons in our world do not offer identifications that permit genuine commitment and engagement, then we must reach beyond these persons. We must learn to live with the uncertainty of creating a new world and endure the tensions of doubt and fear as we struggle to create a beginning that honors our own individuality and selfhood.

C. M.

Upregard . . . Upregard . . . *Upregard?* Well, why not—it is better than *nothingness* . . . nothing happening, nothing being . . . a lump—an uncared for lump—no one knows I'm here—no one knows I exist—I'm not alive—I'm a silent nothingness—so why *not* upregard? I throw it out loudly into the emptiness—it comes back to me; telling me something. Listen! Up . . . Up—life is stirring, oh, deeply, despairingly, but it's there, come on now, *pull*—pull out of the slime of oblivion! But to pull I have to have something to grasp and what is there? There is strength in love—but love has become an ache, a longing. Compassion? I know *that* is there. It seems I feel sorry—sorry for the self I see dying into nothingness —but there is no strength in regrets and no one can help me find it . . . there is just me. I have begun my search. Upregard . . . Upregard!!

JULIE MILLS

Man arises as a unique person through the medium of choice. A good choice is one that is derived authentically: on the basis of self-awareness and self-determined inquiry and action, the person develops the ability to make free and autonomous decisions. The freedom to make choices and to learn from them is the core of being and the basis of all individuality.

C. M.

Strict vine tied me up
   Oppressing, how heavy the feeling is!
I wanted to say, but the voice was
   As thin as a thread,
   Trembling in my throat!

Like a tiny pebble at the bottom
   Of a stream
Covered by an increasing water
   So fast it flowed!

A shadow moved in, another moment,
   "Open your heart."
A smile appeared on a mirror of the water.
The voice touched me,
So did the warmth,
   To make me free!

KAZUKO YOSHINAGA JIBACHI

The definition of me is that I am the one who defines himself. Thus, what I have to do to fulfill my definition is to *define myself*, to answer the question: who am I? And who am I? I am I. This is my definition of myself—pure self-awareness: I am I. The concept I have to fulfill is "I," or, "I am I," and when I fulfill this I am a good I. How do I fulfill this concept? The first thing I found—and many found this is just common philosophy—is that I must not confuse my own intrinsic or moral self with my extrinsic or social self—my inner being with the roles I am playing in society, my fundamental I and the social fractions of me. That's at the bottom of it all. What are the properties that I must fulfill to be I? Well, very simple—be myself. And you? Be yourself. All the words of ethics mean that you should be yourself—and not fool around being anybody else. Sincerity. What does it mean? That you are yourself. Honesty—that you are yourself. Integrity? That you are yourself. Authenticity—"he is an authentic person"—that you are yourself. Is it possible *not* to be yourself? Oh, my God, most of us are not ourselves. We play roles. The word person in Latin meant having a mask in front of yourself. "Persona" means "mask." You play a role—we say we play our role in life. I play the role as professor. You play your role whatever it is. But that's not you. That's playing a role. The you that is yourself is that core of sincerity within you.

ROBERT S. HARTMAN

If learning is to be an alive and vital process, the development of self-awareness is essential. Awareness involves a unity of thought and feeling, here and now; it is a necessary component in the movement toward becoming a person and actualizing oneself. In order to grow in awareness, the individual may have to stop the action, pause, and center directly on himself. What am I feeling at this moment? What is happening within me right now? What is my mood? Do I feel tensions in my body? If I listen carefully, can I actively be in touch with the source of my discontent? What do I want? What do I prefer? How many different levels of awareness can I reach when I am alone? Can I describe each feeling? What thoughts and feelings stand out? Concentrated attention and focusing are initial steps through which awareness develops. In awareness, the person is in touch immediately with inner states. Nathaniel Branden puts it this way:

When a person acts without knowledge of what he thinks, feels, needs or wants, he does not yet have the option of choosing to act differently. That option comes into existence with self-awareness. That is why self-awareness is the basis of change.

When a person becomes self-aware, he is in a position to acknowledge responsibility for that which he does, including that which he does to himself, to acknowledge that he is the cause of his actions—and thus to take ownership of his own life. Self-responsibility grows out of self-awareness.

When a person becomes aware of what he is and takes responsibility for what he does, he experiences the freedom to express his authentic thoughts and feelings, to express his authentic self. Self-assertiveness becomes possible with the achievement of self-awareness and the acknowledgement of self-responsibility.

C. M.

On the rough wet grass of the back yard my father and mother have spread quilts. We all lie there, my mother, my father, my uncle, my aunt, and I too am lying there . . . They are not talking much, and the talk is quiet, of nothing in particular, of nothing at all in particular, of nothing at all. The stars are wide and alive, they seem each like a smile of great sweetness, and they seem very near. All my people are larger bodies than mine . . . with voices gentle and meaningless like the voices of sleeping birds. . . .

By some chance, here they are, all on this earth; and who shall ever tell the sorrow of being on this earth, lying, on quilts, on the grass, in a summer evening, among the sounds of the night. . . .

After a little I am taken in and put in bed. Sleep, soft smiling, draws me unto her; and those receive me, who quietly treat me, as one familiar and well-beloved in that home: but will not, oh, will not, not now, not ever; but will not ever tell me who I am.

JAMES AGEE

"Ma?"

"Yes, Homer?"

"I didn't talk to you last night when I came home, because it was like you said. I couldn't talk. All of a sudden on the way home last night I started to cry. You know I never did cry when I was little or at school when I was in trouble. I always felt ashamed to cry. Even Ulysses never cries. But last night I just couldn't help it, and I don't remember if I was ashamed, even. I don't think I was. And I couldn't come straight home, either. I rode out to Ithaca Wine and then I rode across town to the high school. On the way there I rode past a house where some people had been having a party earlier in the evening—the house was dark now. I took those people a telegram. You know the kind of telegram it was. Then, I went back to town and rode all around the streets looking at everything—all the buildings, all the places I've known all my life, all of them full of people. And then at last I really saw Ithaca and I really knew the people who live in Ithaca. I felt sorry for all of them and I even prayed that nothing would happen to them. After that I stopped crying. I thought a fellow would never cry when he got to be grown up, but it seems as if that's when a fellow starts, because that's when a fellow starts finding out about things." He stopped a moment, and then his voice became even more somber than it had been. "Almost everything a man finds out is bad or sad." He waited a moment for some word from his mother but she didn't speak and didn't turn away from her work. "Why is that so?" he said.

Mrs. Macauley began to speak, still turned away from him. "You'll find out. No one can tell you. Each man finds out for himself, in his own way, because each man is the world."

WILLIAM SAROYAN

If our human purpose is to live and grow and express ourselves, then the chance to grow is everything—for it takes years, even with incalculable love or luck, to walk and wind our own willingness through the whole structure of things. Yet, it is this willingness we can't afford to give up. It is our sole strength, our wish to live! Who gives it up, from fear or force, has to that extent lost himself; he is emasculated (well symbolized by Freud's "castration complex") and sold into slavery and compulsion. He may look like a man, but that is only his body, which he hopes will be fed. How shall he (being less than a man) bridge the gap between discipline and the self-discipline which is choice? How shall he take one step from utter frustration (from self-pity, scorn, greed, guilt or rage) to compassion, generosity and respect? Not by remorse, nor will power, not broken-hearted charity; not by any miracle of "brotherly love" which is not and cannot be in his heart; not by suicide, murder, or the rope trick. Babe or neurotic, he cannot make one step forward because he *cannot want* to. And why in fact should *he* want to, he who sees only the cost and not the gain? (Unwilling renunciation is a kind of suicide and breeds more monsters.) You cannot will yourself to *want* a thing! I know. I've tried for years.

One thing only separates "I should," or "I need," from the simplest "I do want"—and that is not choice but the *freedom to choose.*

Who for that matter would not rather *be himself,* affectionate and free, if he could afford it? No other self is free to feel, to express our nature, to know another and be known. This alone is the human self, that can go out; that can love, and endure, and be loved—because it wants to live.

LETTER TO KAREN HORNEY

There's something inexplicable in me that yearns for expression and growing strength—a sense about life that has always been in me, ever since I can remember feeling and thinking about what life was for, and what I was to give back to life; it is not a selfish sense, rather, an essential sense of life's rich and valuable hold on me, and in many ways, a mysterious communion with life, in which there is a silence filled with creative meanings and imaginings that yearn for concrete expression.

And at the same time, there is a sense of my own limitations in trying to convey the silent meanings of a universe filled to the brim with depth, perspective, alive with a variety of contours, shades, colors, inescapably producing a vision of life itself, where mystery and drama, freeing and prisoned, creative and destructive nuances form themselves in endless patterns of meanings and communications.

PAUL JENSEN

A command rings out within me: "Dig! What do you see?"

"Men and birds, water and stones."

"Dig deeper! What do you see?"

"Ideas and dreams, fantasies and lightning flashes!"

"Dig deeper! What do you see?"

"I see nothing! A mute Night, as thick as death. It must be death."

"Dig deeper!"

"Ah! I cannot penetrate the dark partition! I hear voices and weeping. I hear the flutter of wings on the other shore."

"Don't weep! Don't weep! They are not on the other shore. The voices, the weeping, and the wings are your own heart."

NIKOS KAZANTZAKIS

6

VALUING ONE'S SELF

"Be grateful for yourself. Yes, for yourself. Be thankful. Understand that what a man is is something he can be grateful for, and ought to be grateful for."

WILLIAM SAROYAN

Accept everything about yourself—I mean everything—not some things—everything. Every feeling, idea, hope, fear, smell, appearance—it is you and it is good. . . . You can do anything you choose to do; you can enjoy anything you choose to take part in, to be aware of. You are you and that is the beginning and the end—no apologies, no regrets—you are what you want—because you are you—and who can doubt that—who could want more— you have everything there possibly is—there is no more—you are everything—and you are so large and immense that you could never find the top or bottom—you will spend a lifetime enjoying the search—you will enjoy every minute—there is so much to know and experience within yourself.

JAMES A. GOLD

With smile, and subtle shift of position, they welcomed me into the ongoing dinner conversation. I tried hard to listen, I really did. But it was just the way it always was; I simply couldn't understand what they were saying. It was as if they spoke a foreign language. I never had learned to understand or to speak the social talk that everyone else seems to use as a way of getting along and being friendly.

I couldn't do it as a kid, and I can't do it now. That so very old, so terribly painful shyness was still there, and it still hurt just as much as it ever had. I was, of course, tempted to do my number of putting their whole thing down as superficial and without meaning. But I knew, as I always know, that the bewilderment and emptiness is at that moment mine, not theirs. . . .

That was when I finally got to it. This is just the way it was going to be . . . no matter what, I would always be as painfully shy and as bewildered by the social talk that brings people together, as shy and as bewildered as I had been since I was a kid. Without knowing what you say to leave without hurting, I pushed back my chair, stood up awkwardly, and silently wandered away.

When I awoke I knew, for the first time again, that . . . The shyness is mine, like it or not. It's the best of me and the worst of me, and only the covering it up, the hiding it, and the running from it is not me.

SHELDON KOPP

68

Sing until your breath
Crackles to the last
Note which is caught
Upon the passing wind.
Laugh until the pains
Squeeze authority
Into chaotic blasts
And then into puny puffs.
Cry until the peak of your tears
Like the pure tips of a wave
Before it folds into the
Gulping sea.

Oh, But love when your heart
Beats the beat of nights full
Of Daffodils for then you are.

ANONYMOUS

In the Upanishads there is a story about Yajnavalkya, the sage at a king's court. The king asked him one day, "By what light do human beings go out, do their work and return?" The sage answered, "By the light of the sun." The king then asked, "But when the light of the sun is extinguished, by what light do human beings go out, do their work and return?" The sage said, "By the light of the moon." And so question and answer went on. When the moon is extinguished, man works by the light of the stars; when they are quenched, by the light of fire. And when the light of the fire itself is put out, the king asked, "By what light then can they do their work and still live?" The sage replied: "By the light of the self."

LAURENS VAN DER POST

70

71

7

SELF
AND
OTHERS

1. A significant relationship is unique in all the world. No other is like it. It grows basically out of the peculiarities and differences of the persons involved.

2. The persons in a relationship, as in *The Little Prince*, tame each other.

> *"I cannot play with you," the fox said. "I am not tamed."*
>
> *"Ah! Please excuse me," said the little prince. But after some thought, he added:*
>
> *What does that mean—'tame'?". . .*
>
> *"It is an act too often neglected," said the fox. "It means to establish ties."*
>
> *" 'To establish ties'?"*
>
> *"Just that," said the fox. "To me, you are still nothing more than a little boy who is just like a hundred thousand other little boys. And I have no need of you. And you, on your part, have no need of me. To you, I am nothing more than a fox like a hundred thousand other foxes. But if you tame me, then we shall need each other. To me, you will be unique in all the world. To you, I shall be unique in all the world . . ."*
>
> *"I am beginning to understand," said the little prince.*

In the process of relating, the persons learn to pursue new pathways and to enjoy and value one another's interests and ways. They learn to accept each other's peculiarities and to accommodate in such a way that neither is reduced or compromised but rather each comes to value the new connections and to know and accept the other's special moods and creations.

3. True understanding occurs only after a relationship is formed. Then even single words and body language have meaning. In the absence of a relationship, whatever understanding develops is without real significance.

4. Every genuine relationship contains rituals and patterns that the two persons observe. These distinguish their coming to

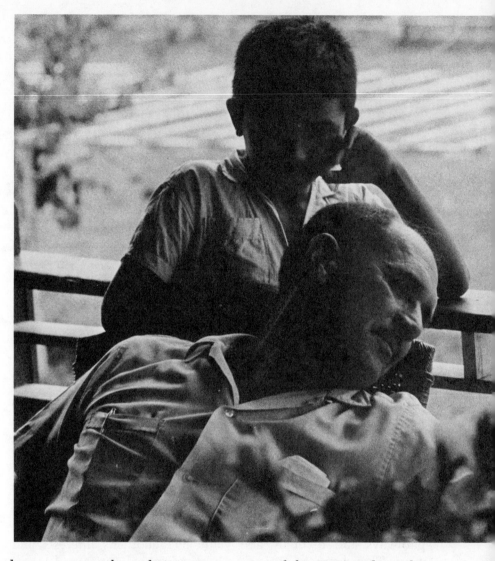

know one another, their unique ways of being together, the making of their life different from all others. Rituals enhance the relationship and turn it into a special and private affair. Early in life the value of rituals is spontaneously realized by many parents who establish special ways of relating with children—rituals that contain a unique flavor no matter how often they are repeated or how crazy they may appear to others. Rituals can continue to hold a particular meaning into adulthood and old age by adding zest, enthusiasm, spirit, and life to meetings with significant others. Some activities in which rituals may be created

and sustained throughout life are story telling, reading poetry, painting together, listening to music, lying quietly side by side, taking a walk, dancing creatively, preparing and sharing special foods, setting aside a regular time to be together, developing unique word forms and body language.

5. Words often are the source of misunderstanding. Silence is sometimes the most effective and powerful way of communicating human presence, involvement, and caring.

6. What is essential in learning and in living is invisible to the eye. What is seen rightly is seen with the heart.

C. M.

The *observer* is wholly intent on fixing the observed man in his mind, on "noting" him. He probes him and writes him up. That is, he is diligent to write up as many "traits" as possible. He lies in wait for them, that none may escape him. . . .

A face is nothing but physiognomy, movements nothing but gestures of expression.

The *onlooker* is not at all intent. He takes up the position which lets him see the object freely, and undisturbed awaits what will be presented to him. Only at the beginning may he be ruled by purpose, everything beyond that is involuntary. . . .

But there is a perception of a decisively different kind. . . .

It is a different matter when in a receptive hour of my personal life a man meets me about whom there is something, which I cannot grasp in any objective way at all, that "says something" to me. That does not mean, says to me what manner of man this is, what is going on in him, and the like. But it means, says something *to me,* addresses something to me, speaks something that enters my own life.

MARTIN BUBER

One does not recognize the otherness of a person as a reality by projecting into him one's fantasies, however flattering they may be. And when one sees in a person one's mother or father or anyone else, one ignores the person as he really is. In the last analysis this is a fundamental disregard for and destructive attitude toward the other person. The understanding of the other person—as we are now using this expression—is not some sort of shrewd "practical psychology" which has a keen eye for the weakness of people, but a deep perception of the core, of the essential nature of the other person.

ANDRAS ANGYAL

The reality of the other person is not in what he reveals to you, but in what he cannot reveal to you.

Therefore, if you would understand him, listen not to what he says but rather to what he does not say.

KAHLIL GIBRAN

We can know the meanings experiences have for others by listening with objectivity and attempting to understand the essence of the experience through the person relating it. Objectivity here refers to seeing what an experience *is* for another person, not how it fits or relates to other experiences—not what causes it, why it exists, or what purpose it serves. It is an attempt to see attitudes and concepts, beliefs and values of an individual as they are to him at the moment he expresses them—not what they were or will become. The experience of the other person as he perceives it is sufficient unto itself, and can be understood in terms of itself alone.

C. M.

I place a great deal of emphasis on people really listening to each other, to what the person has to say, because one seldom encounters a person capable of taking either you or themselves seriously. But I was not really like this when I was out of prison —although the seeds were there, but there was too much confusion and madness mixed in. I was not too interested in communicating with other people—that is not true. What I mean is, I had a profound desire for communicating with and getting to know other people, but I was incapable of doing so, I didn't know how.

ELDRIDGE CLEAVER

So the first simple feeling I want to share with you is my enjoyment when I can really *hear* someone. I think perhaps this has been a long-standing characteristic of mine. I can remember this in my early grammar school days. A child would ask the teacher a question and the teacher would give a perfectly good answer to a completely different question. A feeling of pain and distress would always strike me. My reaction was, "But you didn't *hear* him!" I felt a sort of childish despair at the lack of communication which was (and is) so common.

CARL R. ROGERS

Genuine learning and growth are self-initiated responses to life, expressions of one's own voice, inner experience, desire, preference, feeling. Whether the individual initiates communication or is responding to another, the message is always personal, internal, descriptive and characteristic of the person himself. Relations deepen and grow when persons initiate life and respond to each other. Reactions are helpful in seeking information and in gathering facts, but they do not contribute to personal enhancement or to life. Thus, children should be encouraged to initiate and determine their own learning and to respond with whatever feelings and thoughts are evoked. Practice in initiating and in responding is essential to the development of the self and to learning that is meaningful, exciting, and rewarding.

C. M.

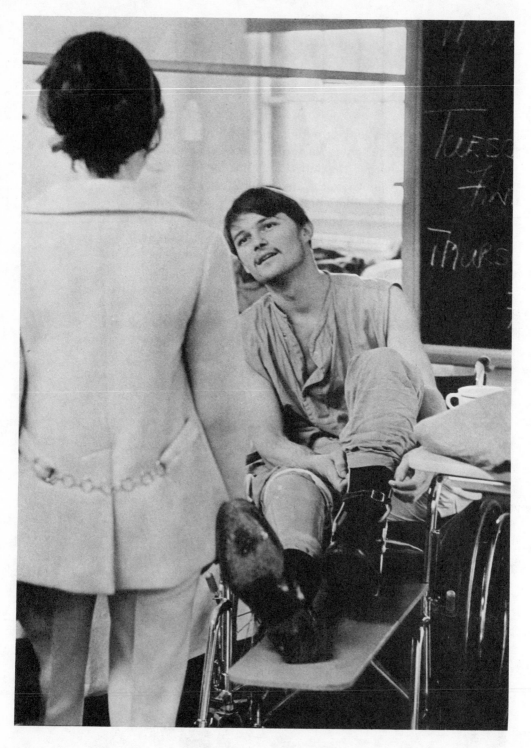

A sense of relatedness to another person is an essential requirement of individual growth. The relationship must be one in which each person is regarded as an individual with resources for his own self-development. Self-growth sometimes involves an internal struggle between dependency needs and strivings for autonomy, but the individual eventually feels free to face himself if he is in a relationship where his human capacity is recognized and cherished and where he is accepted and loved. Then he is able to develop his own quantum in life, to become more and more individualized, self-determining, and spontaneous.

C. M.

When he was about three, Standing Bear would be sent to bring his father's pony to be bridled, and to get the village whetstone—a difficult task, as he had to go from tipi to tipi until he found it. With this came the development of autonomy: there was no supervision; the child was trusted to carry out his responsibility. No external inducement was offered; and in fact, "No one ever said to a child, 'Do this and I will pay you it.'" Neither was coercion used in teaching responsible behavior. "Father . . . never said, 'You have to do this,' or 'You must do that.' But when doing things himself he would often say something like 'Son, some day when you are a man you will do this.'" Coercion, persuasion were never acceptable among the Dakota since no man could decide for another, nor was responsible for the behavior of another.

DOROTHY LEE

No prince could have been more privileged, or had more willing subjects to worship his footsteps, than Barry in the short years that his legs have been long enough and free enough to follow his heart about this place. I have seen him walking across the fields on a sparkling morning with a half dozen dogs, a flock of sheep and his tomcat all bunched behind him as if he were the Pied Piper of Hamelin. I have seen colts follow him so lovingly that he would sometimes stop to wipe their breath from the back of his neck. . . . I have watched the shine of Barry's eyes as he has cupped a day-old chick in his hands and pressed its yellow fluff against the red of his cheek. I have heard him crawling through the chaff and the webs and the dark of the stable loft to find where the cat has hidden her kittens. I have watched him go to sleep, nose to nose with his favorite dog, as if he were determined to keep love beside him all through the night.

Is there any better lesson for a youngster to learn than how to love and be loved?

H. GORDON GREEN

Human beings are not machines that have loose wires in them or burnt-out tubes, that an ideal surgeon can reach and fix, or adjust, or take out, or reconnect. We are interactive, experiential organisms. *When* I respond to what goes on in a person *then* something goes on *in him*. Of course, something goes on in him also before I respond. He is in pain, anxious or dulled; he has lost his sense of himself; he does not have any feelings; everything is flat. When I respond (or let us say, when I succeed in responding, because I often try and fail for weeks and months), then something more is suddenly going on, he does feel something, there is a surprising sense of self and he feels "Gee, maybe I'm not lost.". . .

EUGENE T. GENDLIN

When I sit with someone, I know that *is something*, even if I have nothing valuable to say. I no longer need constant evidence that I am being effective and helpful. I can just sit and give my company. I have been in situations where my pain could not be understood, and I have taken comfort just being with someone willing to *be* with me, someone who required nothing, could not grasp my torn-up feelings but was human company—like a place to go when you are down and out, a human presence, civilization after wilderness. It is a lot when I just sit with someone. But I believe it helps to *say* that I mean to sit in silence. It helps to make it something.

EUGENE T. GENDLIN

. . . the encounter is a meeting of harmony and mutuality, a feeling of being within the life of another person while at the same time maintaining one's own identity and individuality. The encounter is a decisive inner experience in which new dimensions of the self are revealed (not as intellectual knowledge but as integral awareness) and broadening and enlarging values are discovered.

C. M.

In the encounter between adult and child, each person enters into a meaningful tie where mental power and compasssion mingle. No matter how complicated, how discouraging or frightening, no matter how uncertain the process, the possibility for encounter is present when the adult's courage and strength and perceptiveness are available. The life of encounter is a two-way process. It is a person-to-person meeting in which child and adult collaborate in their search to unravel the hidden meanings; to clarify the distortions and confusion; to disclose real feelings and thoughts; to create a climate of learning, where conflicts, challenge, and emerging insight and awareness integrate with sensitivity and compassion in restoring a child to mature and healthy self-hood. New potentialities are actualized in the solitary inner dialogue and in the exquisite fullness of communal life.

C. M.

. . . creative confrontation is a struggle between persons who are engaged in a dispute or controversy and who remain together, face to face, until acceptance, respect for differences, and love emerge; even though the persons may be at odds in terms of the issue, they are no longer at odds with each other. The confrontation is a way to deeper intimacy and relatedness, to authentic life between persons. The persons must be courageous enough to live through the unknown factors in the confrontation, trusting enough to let the breach heal through silent presence and communion when words and dialogue fail, strong enough to maintain a love and respect for each other whatever else may be canceled out in the issue or dispute. The persons never lose sight of the fact that each is seeking in his or her own way, however fragmentary or futile or destructive the way may appear, to find an authentic existence, to find a life of meaning and value, and to express the truth.

C. M.

The threat of anxiety as a *potentiality* can be eliminated only by the *actual encounter* with the dreaded situation or activity, because until we actually meet the situation we do not know whether and how we will be able to live with it, master it, or perish in it, and thus we cannot transform the unknown and new ing something knowable and known. Such encounter means leaving the embeddedness of the familiar and going forth to an unknown meeting with the world. . . . The determination to go forward to such encounters keeps open the doors to an expanding life, while the seeking of protection in the embeddedness of the familiar makes for stagnation and constriction of life.

ERNEST G. SCHACHTEL

. . . What he was seeking was an opponent—and I use the term in its literal sense of someone who is opposite—who would draw from him the full exercise of all that was in him; one who would evoke him—not push or compel him—to an answering response of exertion beyond known limits. The partners he liked usually defeated him. Yet he chose them, because they invited him to actualize all his capacities—his coordination, his split-second judgment, his footwork, his skill, his imagination, his planning. . . . He sought a partner who would engage his whole being to full commitment.

DOROTHY LEE

I have sometimes tried to play for you before, and for some brief periods have had some measure of success, but often just the opposite. It was as though, when I started playing, you wanted to be playing too, and you came to the piano and you banged on it to try to make your tune while I was trying to make mine. It was an un-holistic mess for you and for me. If you wish to play, and I deeply hope you do, you name your time and place and let us join, respecting you as "creating one" for that occasion as now I ask of you for this.

ROSS L. MOONEY

The relational world is individual, yet it is universal. If the self were solely the individual's, it could not be true. At the same time if it were not intimately his, it would not be real. The oneness of each individual realizes itself by uniting with others. There is no concept of man or human nature in which every person is not a part. Love is indivisible between objects and one's own self, and love of one person implies love of man as such, recognizing and nurturing oneself not only for oneself but for all of life. These two elements of selfhood—uniqueness and universality—grow together, until at last the most unique becomes the most universal.

C. M.

Healthy communal life can be established only in a setting in which the person is free to explore his capacities and to discover for himself meanings and values that will enable him to create an identity. We can help a person to be himself by our own willingness to steep ourselves temporarily in his world, in his private feelings and experiences. By our affirmation of the person as he is we give him support and strength to take the next step in his own growth.

C. M.

The individual will learn social values through encounters with significant others and through separation of the self from others. Whether he chooses social values because they confirm basic tendencies within himself depends upon the kind of being he is as well as the nature of his emotional experiences and ties with others. With reference to authentic relatedness, all that one person can do is be there, in an alive, genuine way. To the extent that this presence fits, it will have a bearing on emerging feelings and values. Thus, the individual, in a healthy climate of growth and development, will learn from others, beyond the social amenities and routines, certain values of the self—authenticity, sensitivity, gentleness, kindness, truth, and ways of genuine participation and joint effort.

C. M.

8

COMMUNICATING AND RELATING

What does it mean to know another person in all the regions of the self, to hear the range of voices, the tones and textures and sounds, the variations of speech in early morning and late night and in the many moments between, the sounds of joy, the piercing anger, the sadness and the laughter, the edgy, uncertain words of fear, and all the facial and body expressions—surprise, doubt, shock, terror, rage, madness; lengthy silences and words that seem never to stop flowing, all the ups and downs of ecstasy and misery? The flat, empty sounds and the cold, vacant, almost frozen stares. All the contradictions of inner and outer are present when courage is fear and kindness is dishonesty, when laughter covers tears and sweetness is a form of rage.

Fully to know another person in all the dimensions of the self is a long journey of listening, feeling, sensing, risking, trusting, doubting, joining, fighting, loving, supporting, opposing, laughing, weeping. When it works and two people actually meet and create a full life, then the mutual sense is always present, and the two selves are alive and responsive. Each person experiences the center of self and other and creates vibrations unlike any other sounds or movements. Such a relationship does not follow a tangible form or predictable directions. Its essence is a mystery, happening but once and unrepeatable.

C. M.

A person is either himself or not himself; is either rooted in his existence or is a fabrication; has either discovered what it means to be a unique person is or still playing around with masks and roles and status symbols. And nobody is more aware of this than the person who suddenly realizes that he has been living dishonestly. Only an authentic person can evoke a good response in the core of the other person. Only a real person can resonate in the depths of being with another person.

C. M.

One of the most difficult lessons we, as adults, must learn is to recapture the sense of honesty which was so keen and powerful in childhood. Young children who are not even aware that honesty is a virtue have such a keen sense of speaking directly, truthfully, and openly that even when they are taught to be kind, tactful, and polite, their sense of honesty remains so spontaneous and genuine that they persist in saying what they feel no matter how severe the consequences may be. Only after repeated correction, disapproval, punishment, and rejection does the child submit and learn the gains of distortion, subtlety, and deviation. Only then does the social need for kindness and sympathy, for achievement and reward, for success and approval, exceed the

determination to remain true to one's own eyes and ears and heart.

When we are not honest, we are cut off from a significant resource of ourselves, a vital dimension that is necessary for unity and wholeness. A significant stream of inner life is dammed up, and until we recapture and recreate that sense of honesty we cannot know ourselves and we cannot know other persons and grow as individuals and in relationships.

C. M.

97

What an awesome thing it is to feel oneself on the verge of the possibility of really knowing another person. Can it ever happen? I'm not sure. I don't know that any two people can really strip themselves that naked in front of each other. We're so filled with fears of rejection and pretenses that we scarcely know whether we're being fraudulent or real ourselves.

Of all the dangers we share, probably the greatest comes from our fantasizing about each other. Are we making each other up? We have no way to test the reality of it.

BEVERLY AXELROD

The reason two people are reluctant to really strip themselves naked in front of each other is because in doing so they make themselves vulnerable and give enormous power over themselves one to the other. How awful, how deadly, how castrophically they can hurt each other, wreck and ruin each other forever! How often, indeed, they end by inflicting pain and torment upon each other. Better to maintain shallow, superficial affairs; that way the scars are not too deep, no blood is hacked from the soul. Getting to know someone, entering that new world, is an ultimate, irretrievable leap into the unknown.

ELDRIDGE CLEAVER

We struggled together, knowing. We prattled, pretended, fought bitterly, laughed, wept over sad books or old movies, nagged, supported, gave, took, demanded, forgave, resented— hating the ugliness in each other, yet cherishing that which we were. . . . Will I ever find someone to battle with as we battled, love as we loved, share with as we shared, challenge as we challenged, forgive as we forgave. You used to say that I saved up all of my feelings so that I could spew forth when I got home. The anger I experienced in school I could not vent there. How many times have I heard you chuckle as you remembered the day I would come home from school and share with you all of the feelings I had kept in. "If anyone had been listening they would have thought you were punishing me, striking out at me. I always survived and you always knew that I would still be with you when you were through." There was an honesty about our relationship that may never exist again.

VIAN CATRELL

A *Ritual to Read to Each Other*

If you don't know the kind of person I am
and I don't know the kind of person you are
a pattern that others made may prevail in the world
and following the wrong god home we may miss our
    star.

For there is many a small betrayal in the mind
a shrug that lets the fragile sequence break
sending with shouts the horrible errors of childhood
storming out to play through the broken dyke.

And as elephants parade holding each elephant's tail,
but if one wanders the circus won't find the park,
I call it cruel and maybe the root of all cruelty
to know what occurs but not recognize the fact.

And so I appeal to a voice, to something shadowy,
a remote important region in all who talk;
though we could fool each other, we should consider—
lest the parade of our mutual life get lost in the dark.

For it is important that awake people be awake,
or a breaking line may discourage them back to sleep;
the signals we give—yes or no, maybe—
should be clear; the darkness around us is deep.

WILLIAM STAFFORD

What Shall He Tell That Son?

A father sees a son nearing manhood.
What shall he tell that son?
"Life is hard; be steel; be a rock."
And this might stand him for the storms
    and serve him for humdrum and monotony
    and guide him amid sudden betrayals
    and tighten him for slack moments.
"Life is soft loam; be gentle; go easy."
And this too might serve him.
Brutes have been gentled where lashes failed.
The growth of a frail flower in a path up
    has sometimes shattered and split a rock.
A tough will counts. So does desire.
So does a rich soft wanting.
Without rich wanting nothing arrives.
Tell him too much money has killed men
    and left them dead years before burial;
    and quest of lucre beyond a few easy needs
    has twisted good enough men
    sometimes into dry thwarted worms.
Tell him time as a stuff can be wasted.
Tell him to be a fool every so often
    and to have no shame over having been a fool
    yet learning something out of every folly
    hoping to repeat none of the cheap follies
    thus arriving at intimate understanding
    of a world numbering many fools.
Tell him to be alone often and get at himself
    And above all tell himself no lies about himself,
    whatever the white lies and protective fronts
    he may use amongst other people.

Tell him solitude is creative if he is strong
    and the final decisions are made in silent rooms.
Tell him to be different from other people
    if it comes natural and easy being different.
Let him have lazy days seeking his deeper motives.
Let him seek deep for where he is a born natural.
        Then he may understand Shakespeare
        and the Wright brothers, Pasteur, Pavlov,
    Michael Faraday and free imaginations
bringing changes into a world resenting change.
        He will be lonely enough
        to have time for the work
        he knows as his own.

CARL SANDBURG

A belief in a reality is a condition of its coming into existence. Belief is essential in all growing relationships and can be the condition which enables a person to risk and move forward to new life. In Selwyn James's essay on Conan Doyle, he quotes dialogues with his mother to illustrate the significance of unshakable belief in overcoming obstacles that interfere with purposes and desires.

"Bring back a palm sapling," she once wrote to my father in Africa. Dutifully, he lugged it home. "It will die—it stands to reason," he predicted glumly. Mother planted it anyway—probably the only palm tree to flourish in an English garden.

That same summer, her belief in the impossible was put to its sternest test. My brother's front tooth was knocked out of its socket by a cricket ball. Though he came home bloody and miserable, Mother had no time for his tears, "Where is the tooth?" she inquired calmly. When my brother shrugged, she whisked us all off to the cricket field where we searched until we found it, miraculously whole, in the grass.

Then we rushed with it to the family dentist. "Put it back," Mother demanded.

The startled man tried to protest, but he must have seen my mother's eyes burning bright beyond common sense. He stuck the tooth back in my brother's mouth, braced it to the ones on either side, and stitched the gum. Within months the brace was removed. Defying all dental logic, the tooth stayed rooted for the next 28 years. "See what happens when you believe," Mother used to say tirelessly.

C. M.

"I can't thank you for what you've done and for the kind of human being you are. . . . I couldn't believe anybody could be really decent, because it made my whole feeling about everything any everybody untrue—the feeling I have had for a long time that the human race is hopeless and corrupt, that there isn't one man in the world worthy of another man's respect. For a long time I've had contempt for the pathetic as well as for the proud, and then suddenly thousands of miles from home, in a strange city, I found a man who was decent. It bothered me. It bothered me for a long time. I couldn't believe it. I had to find out. I wanted it to be true. I wanted to believe it, because I've been telling myself for years: 'Let me find one man uncorrupted by the world so that I may be uncorrupted, so that I may believe and live.' I wasn't sure the first time we met, but I'm sure now. I want nothing more from you. You've given me everything I want. You can't give me anything more. You understand, I know. When I get up it shall be to say good-by. You needn't worry about me. I'm going home where I belong. I'm not going to die of this sickness. I'm going to live. And now I'm going to know *how* to live."

WILLIAM SAROYAN

What is required of us in our time
is that we go down
into uncertainty
where what is new is old as every morning,
and what is well known is not known as well:

That we go down
into the most human
where living men have vanished
and the music of their meaning
has been trapped and sealed.

What is asked of us in our time
is that we break open
our blocked caves
and find each other.
Nothing less will heal the anguished spirit,
nor release the heart to act in love.

RAYMOND JOHN BAUGHAN

106

9

LOVE IN RELATIONSHIPS

We always grew together
In the words we chose and
In the silence of our
Affirmation of each other.

We always held our ground
    When the machines moved in
    And tried to uproot us
    From gentle paths that sometimes
        ended nowhere.

We always loved each other
    When we walked in places
        long forgotten
    And spoke in rooms
    That sang our songs.

We lived, and laughed,
    and created vibrant melodies
        in a world that we made new.

C. M.

Love creates an embracing meaning in relationship. It gives
the life of the person a sense of value, a feeling of goodness. Love
is a force that nourishes growth. It is the sunshine and the seed
but it is not growth itself. To grow, one needs the soil and the rain
as well as the seeds of love. Love endures the test of crisis,
tragedy, the changes of time. It is the source from which other
things come: tears and laughter; fear and courage; anger and con-

tentment; restlessness and tranquility. Thus, love is ultimate, complete in itself while other qualities require the presence of love to attain a sense of value.

C. M.

In the final words of Archibald MacLeish's play *J. B.*:

We can never know . . .
He answered me like the . . .
                     stillness of a star
That silences us, asking.
We *are* and that is all our answer
We are and what we are can suffer . . .
But . . .
        what suffers, loves . . .
               and love
Will live its suffering again,
Risk its own defeat again,
Endure the loss of everything again
And yet again and yet again
In doubt, in dread, in ignorance, unanswered,
Over and over, with the dark before,
The dark behind it . . .
            and still live . . .
                 still love.

Can you sometimes
just come
and hold me
to make me feel
a child again,
dependent again,
taken care of again?

I am not strong
as I seem,
nor self-sufficient
as I choose to seem.
Can you help me
to learn
to depend upon you
and let me
lean on you
sometimes
just a little bit?

I don't want words
nor promises—
the peace of a child
knowing he is loved
cared for
and held—
silently.

MINÉ AKANLAR BOYD

111

In the creative relationship, changes occur not because one person deliberately sets out to influence and alter the behavior or attitude of another person but because it is inevitable that when individuals really meet as persons and live together in a fundamental sense they will modify their behavior so that it is consistent with values and ideals which lead to self-realizing ends. The creative relationship is an experience of mutual involvement, commitment, and participation, a meeting of real persons. It can be studied or learned in a static and discrete sense, but it can be known only through living.

C. M.

So Agatha spoke about golf and about the love men have for one another.

"It's the only reason ye play at all," she said. "It's a way ye've found to get together and yet maintain a proper distance. I know you men. Yer not like women or Italians huggin' and embracin' each other. Ye need tae feel yer separate love. Just look—ye winna come home on time if yer with the boys. I've learned that o'er the years. The love ye feel for your friends is too strong for that. All those gentlemanly rools of affection—all the waitin' and oohin' and ahin' o'er yer shots, all the talk o' this ones drive and that one's putt and the other one's gorgeous swing—what is it all but love? Men lovin' men, that's what golf is."

MICHAEL MURPHY

112

What for me is the beginning
may not be the beginning for you,
but you're right about us.

Life will be different because
you are, I am.

We bring the not-yet into being,
and if we don't we lose
in what we take from us,
in how we take the future from
ourselves.

RAYMOND JOHN BAUGHAN

Strange, at this moment as I write I feel only your presence, not an image or memory, not a far-away picture of you in a distant land, but only you, now, in an alive and vigorous sense.

Friendship between us did not just suddenly form, all at once, whole and complete—yet I still remember vividly that day long ago when we screamed with glee, when he discovered each other. That day we opposed the forces of power, the rules and conventions, and all the machinelike people; all the things they were pushing us to do. Something great and wonderful happened when we realized each other. We walked out together, conversing and laughing, leaving the others open-mouthed, puzzled at what our union was all about. Nothing else mattered but the joy of our meeting. Their details, their policies, their words and pronouncements—nothing touched us for we were experiencing an awareness and knowing that had no bounds.

From that day, how many times we stood by what we believed in spite of the consequences. We shared hilarity and sorrow; we shared compassion and indignation.

The pattern we established in that first meeting expanded and grew, in silence, in forceful words, in struggles to write poems and in other forms of self-expression.

Remember those fresh walks along the path, the early morning coffee, that bright beginning of the day, with the smell of flowers in the back seat of the car and the smell of books wherever we went? With us there was always a flavor, a style, a particular shape of life, an exciting variety of smells, and colors, and forms.

What has it all meant? For me it is clear—the creation of a friendship, spontaneity, immediacy, vigor in everything we shared; a life of openness, directness, and honesty of expression. It remains here with me, alive in a very special way, in my solitary hours, fond memories, an inner spirit of joy, and always, with you, love.

C. M.

114

To recognize and to accept the otherness of a person means to respect him as a valuable being in his own right, in his independence. This attitude is incongruous with any idea of possessiveness or any tendency to use him as means to an end, be this in the form of exploitation, domination, or some other attitude. In other words, it is incongrous with the nature of love to try to reduce the loved person to "an item in one's personal world," or to try to make him comply with one's demands, or to try to exert power over him in whatever way. Love has to be recognized as a basic human attitude which is quite distinct from and irreducible to man's self-assertive tendencies.

ANDRAS ANGYAL

somewhere i have never travelled

somewhere i have travelled, gladly beyond
any experience, your eyes have their silence:
in your most frail gesture are things which enclose me,
of which i cannot touch because they are too near

your slightest look easily will unclose me
though i have closed myself as fingers,
you open always petal by petal myself as Spring opens
(touching skilfully, mysteriously) her first rose

or if your wish be to close me, i and
my life will shut very beautifully, suddenly,
as when the heart of this flower imagines
the snow carefully everywhere descending;

nothing which we are to perceive in this world equals
the power of your intense fragility: whose texture
compels me with the colour of its countries,
rendering death and forever with each breathing
(i do not know what it is about you that closes
and opens; only something in me understands
the voice of your eyes is deeper than all roses)
nobody, not even the rain, has such small hands

E. E. CUMMINGS

116

I have chosen to be alone, to respect my own inner life and to pursue my own sense of direction.

I have chosen to be with others, in utter silence, in dialogue, in wide ranges of color, texture, movement, sound, taking the path of the heart, trusting invisible messages, forever and always believing in each person's potential for growing, in each person's right to find himself and to find others.

I have chosen to live, to infuse my spirit into each human venture, to risk myself in the hope of knowing the glory of a voice that speaks for the first time, of witnessing the birth of individuality, of seeing energy and spirit suddenly merging into new activities and forms, of sparking and sustaining a light from within that continues to glow even in darkness.

C. M.

(continued from page vi *)*

"Mother to Son" taken from *Selected Poems* by Langston Hughes. Published by Alfred A. Knopf, Inc.

"My Precious Gift from Conan Doyle" by Selwyn James. From *Northwestern Evening Mail.*

The Saviors of God by Nikos Kazantzakis. Copyright 1960. Published by Simon and Schuster, Inc.

The Sickness Unto Death by Soren Kierkegaard. Published by Princeton University Press.

If You Meet the Buddha on the Road, Kill Him! by Sheldon Kopp. Science and Behavior Books, Ben Lomond, California, 1972.

"Violence and Love" by R. D. Laing. *Journal of Existentialism* 1965, #5.

J. B. by Archibald MacLeish. Published by Houghton Mifflin Co.

"Self-Actualizing People" by A. H. Maslow. From *Symposium #1 1950 Values in Personality Research* edited by Werner Wolff, Copyright 1950 by Grune & Stratton, Inc.

"Some Educational Implications of the Humanistic Psychologies" by A. H. Maslow. *Harvard Educational Review* Fall 1968, Volume 38.

Creativity and Conformity by Clark Moustakas, 1967. Reprinted by permission of D. Van Nostrand Company.

The Authentic Teacher by Clark Moustakas, 1966. Reprinted by permission of Howard A. Doyle Publishing Co.

Human Potentialities by Gardner Murphy. Published by Basic Books, Inc. 1958.

Golf and the Kingdom by Michael Murphy. Published by Viking Press, 1973.

Freedom To Learn: A View of What Education Might Become by Carl Rogers. Published by C. E. Merrill Publishing Co., 1969.

"Toward a Modern Approach to Values: The Valuing Process in the Mature Person." by Carl Rogers. Taken from *Journal of Abnormal and Social Psychology* Volume 68, #2, 1964.

"a father sees a son nearing manhood" by Carl Sandburg. From *The People, Yes* by Carl Sandburg, copyright 1936 by Harcourt Brace Jovanovich, Inc., renewed 1964 by Carl Sandburg. Reprinted by permission of the publisher.

The Little Prince by Antoine de Saint-Exupéry. Copyright 1943, 1971 by Harcourt Brace Jovanovich, Inc. and reprinted with their permission.

Human Comedy by William Saroyan. Copyright 1943, 1971 by William Saroyan. Reprinted by permission of Harcourt Brace Jovanovich, Inc.

Metamorphosis by Ernest G. Schachtel. Published by Basic Books, Inc., 1959.

"A Ritual To Read To Each Other" by William Stafford. First appeared in *Hudson Review*.

The Heart of the Hunter by Laurens van der Post. Published by Wm. Morrow and Co.

How People Change by Alan Wheelis. Published by Harper & Row, Inc. 1973.

"A Report of a Recorded Interview in the Course of Psychotherapy" by Otto Will and Robert H. Cohen. Taken from *Psychiatry* #16, 1953.

Finally, I thank the photographers and artists whose work provides the vivid illustrations that bring to the written material an additional dimension of what it means to be alone and with others: Lesley Abugov —Bethel Agency, Lynn Bentley-Kemp, James Crawford, Eileen Christelow, Ron Diamond—Bethel Agency, Ed Eckstein, Nancy Flowers—Bethel Agency, Donna Harris—The Merrill-Palmer Institute, Marcia Kay Keegan, David Krasnor, Lester Lunsky, Elizabeth Margaritis—Bethel Agency, Alan Samilijan, and Erika Stone.

Pictorial Credits

Nancy Flowers/Bethel Agency: pages 2, 11, 25, 41, 71, 74-75
David Krasnor/Bethel Agency, page 5
James Crawford, page 8
Donna Harris, pages 15 (left), 77, 85
Erika Stone/Bethel Agency, pages 15 (right), 53, 81, 110
Lester Lunsky, page 20
Lesley Abugov/Bethel Agency, pages 23, 95
Ed Eckstein/Bethel Agency, pages 30, 82, 117
Lynne Bentley-Kemp, pages 33, 47, 68
Ron Diamond/Bethel Agency, pages 51, 62-63, 101
Eileen Christelow/Bethel Agency, page 70
Elizabeth Margaritis/Bethel Agency, page 79
Alan Samilijan, page 88
Marcia Kay Keegan/Bethel Agency, page 97